D1827781

"You can only change

yourself"

INDEX

Cartoons:	Dirk Stallaert
Cover:	Andreas Ruhland
Editing:	Victoria Walsh
Lay Out/design:	Dick Hofman
Graphs:	Loek Otters
Print office:	Ton Clement

Copies of **Oops! I'm the Boss** can be ordered through the website www.mayventures.nl.

The website also contains details of Henno's seminars and workshops on leadership and change management.

First Edition January 2010
ISBN/EAN: 978-90-815161-1-2

© Henno Janmaat
All Rights Reserved

Henno Janmaat

Henno Janmaat took a quite different career path to most of his friends who also went into business. Within the multinationals he has worked for (a large bank and a large energy company), he has always looked for positions with the highest level of autonomy. For young people in large corporate enterprises, the highest level of autonomy is usually in general management positions in small and medium-sized daughter companies.

Over the years, Henno has worked on approximately 15 hands-on turn-around processes. He has specialised in bringing loss-making companies back on track, by focussing on motivating instead of giving orders. Between 2007 and 2010, Henno was Director of Westland Energie, a business with a one billion Euro turnover, selling power and gas both business-to-business and business-to-consumers. In 2007, the company was making a loss, but by the end of 2009 it was making a solid profit and was awarded the prize for the best energy company in the Netherlands (GfK Award).

In 2010, Henno started his own business, again bringing loss-making companies back on track, working as an interim manager. In addition to that, Henno speaks at seminars and holds workshops on leadership and change management. He graduated from the Erasmus University in 1997 and is married with a young son.

Once asked what his personal 'brand' would be, Henno answered that it would be a combination of "Le Penseur" (the Rodin statue) and Mick Jagger of the Rolling Stones. This is because Henno combines an enormous interest in why things are how they are, with a strong wish to entertain.

Henno strongly believes one cannot change other people, but can only change oneself. However, by changing oneself, one can have an enormous impact on the rest of the world.

THE NEW MANAGER

Prologue

I will never forget my first day as the head of a company. I was so proud! Finally, I was going to do what I had always dreamed of. The week before, I had called all my friends; the evening before I had sipped champagne with my family. I felt ready for it. I entered the building with polished shoes, a new tie, a new briefcase and all the self-confidence in the world. This was my chance. I was going to live my dream.

As I passed through the entrance hall, I noticed an irate-looking man standing at the reception desk. Walking up the stairs to my office, where a bouquet of fresh flowers was waiting for me, I heard the man shouting at the receptionist: "I want to see the goddamn imbecile that's in charge of this #$%@$$# company". Settling into my cosy new leather chair, surveying my clean, smart office, and smelling the lovely flowers, I suddenly realised: "Damn, the guy he's looking for .... that's me".

Oops! I'm the Boss. It dawned on me that I didn't have a clue what to expect or how to behave as the head of a new team. How do I start, what should I do, what should I ask, what should I focus on?

Over the years, I have looked for a simple, practical guide to dealing with this kind of situation. I have tried to find something that gives an overview of what one might expect and outlines best practice for starting with a new team. I never found a suitable book, so I decided to write one myself.

In this book, I share all my experiences that might be relevant for getting up to speed with new teams. I have drawn on experiences from my business and personal life. Some are serious, some are more light-hearted, but they all focus on creating an environment for continuous improvement, and on building a high-performing organisation within a limited timeframe.

The book contains 53 'columns', each containing a different topic, with one for each week of the first year with your new team (yep, some years do have 53 weeks). The columns are designed to be easy to read, but may be difficult to implement. Discussing the columns with others should help you to identify the best way to lead your team to success. At the time of writing, I was CEO of Westland Energie. I wrote this book in English because I gathered most of my experience outside of Holland. Every story in this book is a story within a specific context, and every new context might require a different approach. Many other approaches might be as successful, or even more successful. This is simply a summary of my experiences, collated to share with you.

I do hope you will enjoy reading this as much as I have enjoyed writing it,

Henno

INTRODUCTION TO THE MANAGER'S STAKEHOLDERS

THE EMPLOYEE

THE CUSTOMER   THE MANAGER'S BOSS

"Sharing is the basis for growth, and you always get something back"

1. Share your insights

Sharing knowledge multiplies its effect. Thinking back to my school days, I remember two kinds of people. There were the ones who shared their information, and the ones who shielded their work with their arms, hiding and protecting what was theirs.

Sharing is the basis for growth, and you always get something back. It might be inspiration, new energy, some new insights, a thicker skin, a new friend, a simple "thanks", or just the wonderful warm feeling that comes from helping others.

GOOD LEADERS START YOUNG

I visit my peers in other companies on a regular basis. Before these meetings, I put together a binder containing my most important insights, which I leave behind after the meeting. The contents of the binder does not vary too much from company to company, since managers deal with the same questions all around the globe.
It tackles questions such as how do you handle mission/vision/strategy, how does your planning and control cycle work, how do you create the right atmosphere for continuous improvement, how do you increase employee satisfaction, how do you best motivate your team, how do you involve your key customers in big changes, etc.

▶

The great thing about sharing in this way is that the people I visit are usually surprised by the fact that I'm sharing my complete toolbox. They are also surprised that it's all written down (other than the confidential stuff), so they don't need to take notes. Because of this openness, the people I visit start to share their insights, tips and tricks with me. They do this partly to return the favour, but partly (and there is an interesting competitive side to this) since everybody wants to show that they too have some good insights.

Every time I have been on such a visit, I have gone home inspired, changed and dying to go to work next day to try some new stuff. I even advise all my employees to do the same thing: summarise what you do (which is an interesting process on its own) and contact someone who does a similar job. Ask them if it's okay to drop by to share information for free, then start presenting and get inspired - all for the price of spending only sixty minutes.

This book is the extended version of my current binder. I'd like to share this with you and hope we will meet some day and exchange insights.

Q: Who would you go to to share your insights?

"People will improve themselves and their company on a continuous basis when they have fun and feel free"

2. Performance by trust

Watching my son grow up, I have learnt three important lessons:
1. he wants to have fun;
2. he wants to improve himself continuously; and
3. he doesn't like being told what to do by his parents.

Transferring this to business life, my team at work decided to experiment with this insight during our budgeting process, as we set our targets and held our monthly performance meetings.

Our old planning and control cycle was a standard one. Targets were set top-down, with superiors cascading their targets, after which endless discussions and poor performance followed. Trying to implement the insights I got as a father, we developed the 'performance by trust' method in our team.

I asked my team members the question: "Who here doesn't have the ambition to improve as a person and to improve our company continuously?" Nobody raised a hand. After a while I continued, saying: "Fine, from now on, I trust you and I will not challenge you on your ambition for next year. Set your own budget, targets and performance indicators, and let's meet in two weeks' time to share the plans".

The format for sharing plans was to evaluate next year's target against this year's latest estimate. Every team member presented his or her own plan, and nobody came back with a plan that did not involve considerable improvement. Some people even showed too much ambition. I can tell you that challenging your people on the reasons for having too much ambition is much pleasanter than the other way around! Freedom and trust energised the troops. The team was so ambitious that the cumulated results met the targets I had been given by my boss (a traditional thinker).

During the year, my team meets for an hour a month, in a meeting that we call the performance board. Each team member presents his or her performance, actual versus budget. When the actual is behind the budget, the specific manager presents the actions that should ensure we reach our targets towards year-end.

My team members feel they are running their own shop. We have all the fun in the world as a team, and our financial performance has never been better. People will improve themselves and their company on a continuous basis when they have fun and feel free. For employees, the pressure of being trusted is much more effective than the pressure of being bossed around. That's equally as true for grown-ups as it is for children.

Q: How do you show your direct reports that you trust them?

"Being a good leader is more about asking the right questions than giving the right answers; more about coaching than giving orders"

3. A good leader is a good facilitator

When I took charge of my first team, I thought I should be smarter than the rest. I thought that being the smartest would make the team respect me and let me lead. Wrong! After a while, I noticed that team members stopped looking at me in meetings when I was talking and did not follow my commands at all. In many cases, they even seem to take pleasure in going in the exact opposite direction.

I found out that it was not about showing my team that I was the smartest, but about making sure that the team members could do what they wanted to do, to explore and achieve their dreams. It was more about asking the right questions than giving the right answers; more about coaching than giving orders. I needed only to make sure that there was alignment on the common goals. After that, it was all about facilitating the team members to reach their own goals.

Ask your team members how you can help them to be successful in their day-to-day work. Ask them where they want to be in a few years' time and what they expect from you to support their development. Ask them what they think your role in the company should be and what you should focus on internally and externally.

If you make your team happy, the team will make you happy, by allowing you to be their leader. A leader can only be a real leader when the team tolerates its leader. It is all about trust. Trust your people and do what they want instead of forcing them to do what you want. Trust your people and you will be trusted. Challenge them on their thoughts, but only overrule them when absolutely necessary. A good leader is a good facilitator.

Q: Where does each of your team members want to be in three years' time?

"Fear has an immediate impact,

but fun creates lasting motivation"

4. Fun versus fear

What is the best way to motivate people? A senior manager once told me a nice anecdote to explain his view on the effect of fear versus the effect of fun. He asked me the following question:

"Suppose two athletes compete in the 100-meter sprint, on the first day of a two-day tournament. The respective coaches have different views on motivating their runners. The first coach decides to let a mean, hungry dog chase his athlete. The second coach positions a gorgeous actress (his athlete's favourite) on the finishing line. Which athlete will win the race: the one who will run to make sure he doesn't get bitten, or the one who has a fantastic incentive for winning the race?"

I said I would think about it. I asked a few male colleagues this same question, and they immediately said they were sure the person who ran for the girl would win the race, though they admitted that being chased by a dog would not be fun. However, as a child, I was once chased by a dog, and the speed I reached really surprised me – boy did I run fast! My answer to the senior manager was that the athlete chased by the dog would win the race, and that I knew this from experience.

The manager then asked me whether I went back to the street where the incident had happened. I replied that I didn't do so for weeks. "Well, that is exactly the difference", he said. "The athlete with the dog chasing him will win this particular race, but he won't come back the next day to run the next race, since he will have lost passion for running. Therefore, the other athlete will win the tournament".

Fear has an immediate impact, but fun creates lasting motivation. I strongly believe that having fun together is the best way to be successful as a team. After all, business is a tournament and not a single race.

Q: How do you motivate people to get from A to B?

"There is always a strongest and a weakest player"

5. Evaluating people against targets alone is too limited

During my youth I played field hockey. I once discussed with my team coach why we always took thirteen players to a match, although we only needed eleven to play (field hockey is played eleven against eleven). In addition to the obvious reason (i.e. having two substitutes), he said he did it because he liked to substitute the best player a few minutes before the end of the match. In Dutch culture, this is the biggest compliment you can get as a player, because it means you get a round of applause from the audience, just for you.

The interesting thing about this approach was that the coach would always substitute the best player whether we were winning or losing. Even if all thirteen players were in better shape than last year, and even if they were all performing way better than anticipated, two players would always be substitutes.

After every game, the coach would take time to talk with the substitutes. He told them that they were not necessarily performing below target, but that the other players were just performing better. Together with the coach, the substitutes would draw up a plan to help them improve their performance and become a core team player. Within the hockey team, we all knew that two of us would sit on the bench each match.

Years later, I understood that this lesson was my first introduction to the philosophy of differentiating independent from the total results. Even if nobody meets their targets, there is always a strongest and a weakest player. The same goes the other way. even if everyone meets their targets, there still is always a strongest and a weakest player. My coach was benchmarking us not only against our personal targets but also against the rest of the team.

Right from the start, he decided on the number of strongest and weakest players, and we all knew that. We were all highly motivated to play, and when we did not play, we sat together with the coach or some senior teammates, who helped us to improve and develop, and to get back in the game. I try to use the same approach in my business life.

Q: Would you determine the percentage of strongest and weakest players in your team?

"It really helps if your employer knows your aspirations for your next career step, so don't share them too late"

6. Express your career ambitions at the right time

An important driver in building a career is expressing your ambition at the right time and in the right way. I know this from (bad) experience! At the beginning of my career, I once expressed a desire for promotion just because a colleague had been promoted. Terribly bad timing!

I have learnt that it is better to choose my own moment, at a time when I feel comfortable in my job, but I know I still need some years' experience to reach the next level. I then ask my boss for a talk on my development, ambition and future. During the meeting, I express my ambition and ask what I need to focus on and develop to be ready to operate at the next level in two years' time.

The worst thing that has happened to me when I have taken this approach is that on one occasion my boss started to laugh, saying that it would be almost impossible for me to reach the next level within two years. I stayed calm and asked why. He explained to me that I lacked experience in several areas and that some of my competencies were still underdeveloped. I asked my boss if he would like to help me to gain those experiences and to work on the improvement of my weaker competencies. He agreed.

As it turned out, the unattainable job became available within six months instead of two years. Funnily enough, my boss told me he was sure I was ready for it, and so I got the promotion I wanted. This was partly because I had worked on the topics that we discussed, but mainly because the company had started to see me as someone who wanted to climb the ladder and was willing to work for it.

It really helps if your employer knows your aspirations for your next career step, so don't share them too late.

Q: Does your boss know your career aspirations?

"Managing by walking round and being visible helps me to understand peoples' needs"

7. Face-time

I'm not sure who invented the title 'head' of a company, but I really like the term and take it very literally. When you are the head of a company or heading a team, people want to see your face. There are a number of ways to do this.

I like to take an hour a day to walk through the office, not with a particular goal, just having a chat here and there. Often, I talk to people about non-business related matters. I enjoy making that round, and I get the feeling the teams like it as well. I try to make it as easy as possible to contact me by walking through the office. While walking (and joking) around, some specific business issues always pop up. However, I don't plan to discuss business beforehand, and this ensures that I am as open and approachable as possible.

The line between spying and showing interest is thin. I try not to do too much business stuff. Middle management runs the business and they would not like me to interfere in their affairs. I would certainly not like my boss to interfere in mine. I fully trust my team members, otherwise they wouldn't be in my team. I just walk around to be visible and approachable, and to create a positive atmosphere by having fun, making compliments on peoples' work and showing interest in their private lives.

Every Friday I have a lunch in my room with three randomly chosen employees. I use the alliteration 'Henno's Hotdogs' for this special hour, which has become my favourite hour of the week. I will keep on doing this in any new jobs I do in future, since it is such a nice way to get to know each other. I can only advise everybody to do a similar thing. I have heard other people doing the same thing, calling it Hank's Hamburger, MD Tea or Mister Tea, for instance. It's a fantastic way to get to know your people, explain why you did this or that, explain once again the company's reason for being, to stress the company's 'tone of voice' (the corporate culture, values and expected behaviours), maybe ask some feedback on new ideas, and preferably have a few laughs with your colleagues.

Being visible doesn't always have to be done in person: it can also mean keeping your staff informed through other means. In addition to the regular company newsletter, I send around a one-pager containing the hottest company news at least once a month.

A friend of mine once taught me a head has TWO ears, TWO eyes and only ONE mouth – in other words, 80% of the senses of the head (of a company) are for input (e.g. listening and looking), and only 20% for output (e.g. communicating). I like that a lot. It helps me focus on really trying to understand what is going on. Managing by walking around and being visible helps me to understand peoples' needs.

Q: How do you ensure you are visible enough?

"Involving employees helps to ensure swift resolution of crises"

8. Stakeholder involvement during a crisis

A few years ago, I was asked to become interim manager of a company that had just entered a huge crisis. The company just lost its most important customer in the B2B segment, amounting to one third of turnover and margin. This experience taught me that involving employees during a crisis helps ensure its swift resolution.

In order to resolve the crisis, we formed three teams. The teams had five members each, including both internal and external people. Each team went through the same brainstorm workshop to come up with solutions to get the company out of the crisis. We also formed an evaluation team (consisting of internal people only) to prioritise all the ideas.

Some ideas (e.g. installing an ideas box, improving communication) were hard to quantify but qualitatively good. Others (e.g. laying people off, moving to a cheaper building, reducing salaries) were easier to quantify but less popular with staff. For each idea, we worked out the associated costs and benefits and the time it would take to implement. Unfortunately, the evaluation team concluded that we had to take unpleasant measures to get the company out of trouble. They came up with two options:

1. Lay off some of the staff; and
2. Reduce all salaries and shift people from Operations to Sales

We organised a meeting with the staff council, the trade union and all the employees to discuss the alternatives. One third of the employees voted for reducing salaries and two thirds voted for redundancies. We concluded that we would use a combination of the two options, and this approach received the backing of the staff council, trade union and all employees. The company got back on track within a few months.

Q: How would you involve your key stakeholders when solving a crisis?

"Think hard about development points when someone is doing well, and about compliments when someone is under-performing"

9. Balance feedback during evaluations

For me, one-to-one performance evaluations are the most important moments between me and my team members. Such an evaluation should be well prepared, thorough and honest. If the individual's targets have been set properly there shouldn't be any surprises in the evaluation, and the nature of the appraisal should be clear before the meeting. However, you, as a leader, can have great impact in these moments.

I have experienced that balancing positive and negative feedback makes for a very productive discussion. I always try to balance the number of compliments against the pieces of advice that I give. For instance, four compliments also mean four tips to become even better. This forces me to think very hard about development points when someone is doing well, or about compliments when someone is under-performing. I have noticed that both under-performers and over-performers like the approach.

Over-performers like it because they normally only hear how well they are doing (it makes a nice change!). Over-performers like to become even better, so they love tips. Under-performers mostly know they are under-performing and are pleasantly surprised when you come up with compliments. If you do it the right way, you might give the under-performer that little extra motivation needed to improve his or her performance, and even to have fun in the process.

▶

In our company, we use a matrix to plot our staff's performance and potential. In addition to my direct reports, I like to pay special attention to the under-performers and the 'high potentials' working for my direct reports. I ask both the under-performers and high potentials to write down, in no more than one page, who they really are, what their strengths and weaknesses are, where they want to be in three years' time, and what they think they still need to develop to fulfil their ambition. Doing this in one page is, I think, much tougher than writing a book!

If I suspect they do not have a good self-image, I help them to get in contact with people that are doing exactly what they want to be doing in three years' time. In this way, they hear from others what they need to be doing to become more successful. Afterwards, they often come to me and tell me exactly what I wanted to tell them, only now they have found it out themselves.

Another thing we do when evaluating our staff is a round of compliments and tips within the team. We ask each team member to give one compliment and one tip to each other team member (in written form). Once everyone has received written input, we each design a small personal development plan. In the next team meeting, everyone presents his or her personal development plan. The feedback is more complete and balanced than when it only comes from me. It is also more fun both for the team and its leader.

Q: Who are the over- and under-performers in your company/team?

10

"An 'all-hands' meeting provides a fantastic overview of the company's business, its people and its current challenges and successes"

10. My favourite set up for an 'all hands' meeting

Most companies I have worked with tend to bring all their employees together on a periodic basis for a plenary meeting, combining business with fun. In my company we tend to call these meetings 'all hands' meetings. We copied this from the Navy, where they say "all hands on deck" when they need everybody to come together. In the Navy this generally implies some kind of emergency, but in our company it's just an opportunity to meet and share thoughts.

All hands meetings are a strange phenomenon. If, as a leader, you do not organise them, some people will complain, but if you do have them, others will complain. I have never managed to have an all hands meeting which everybody liked from start to finish. However, I have experimented with several formats in several situations and would like to share my favourite one. This version is appropriate for a company where it's 'business as usual'.

The idea behind our concept is to increase the insight of staff into each other's work and life. The basic structure is ten presentations of ten minutes, given by ten different employees, in combination with a leisure activity organised by and around a specific passion of one or more employees (for instance: football, music, acting, etc.). The first ten minutes of the ten times ten minutes is for the Managing Director. In these ten minutes, he or she explains the company's reason for being. He sets the tone for the day and reveals the theme of the day. After this, we highlight some recent good work by staff and welcome new employees.

▶

After the first block of ten minutes, we usually ask non-management colleagues to present the rest of the blocks. In this way, people who don't normally lead meetings have the chance to present themselves and their departments. I have seen many colleagues get an enormous energy boost from giving a presentation for the first time in their life. In ten times ten minutes, the audience gets a fantastic overview of the company's business, its people, and its current challenges and successes.

We try to have as many different departments present as possible. We prefer two blocks of five presentations (ending with the most powerful ones). To increase quality and reduce duplication, we do a dry run with all those presenting a few days before the meeting.

After the business presentations (which last from 16:00-18:00), we present the people's passion.

We always link the location of the day to the passion of the day. For instance, we have had meetings in a studio (music), a stadium (football) and a theatre (acting). The colleagues expressing their passion organise the programme for the day. There is nothing better than seeing people present their passion. These colleagues always change in the eyes of the rest of the team in a very positive way.

We end the day with a small buffet or barbeque and invite other colleagues to organise the next all hands meeting. It is nice to see which people and departments take an active role. The first two-three times are a bit hard, but afterwards the event goes like clockwork.

Q: How would you set up an all hands meeting?

"Successful global companies try to copy the customer intimacy of small enterprises"

11. Customer segmentation

In many mid-sized Business-to-Business (B2B) companies, the interaction of senior management with customers is low. In smaller companies (with less than 50 Full Time Equivalents - FTEs), the leader knows exactly who his key customers are. He is involved in the relationship with them, he knows where he is making his margin, who his high potential customers (future growers) are, who he want to collaborate with in terms of strategic developments, and he definitely doesn't serve non-profitable customers.

In most successful big companies of the world, this works in the same way. The only difference is that the CEO of a smaller company knows exactly what to do by heart, by instinct. The biggest companies have enormous orchestrated programmes to facilitate good customer segmentation and higher management involvement, but the underlying principles are the same. Successful global companies try to copy the customer intimacy of small enterprises.

Many of the companies in the mid segment struggle with customer segmentation and higher management involvement in the commercial process. Good customer segmentation means you know what you earn on a specific relationship (ultimately the most important driver behind the commercial relationship). In addition to profitability (including credit risk), many other factors can determine the attractiveness of the relationship. You can think of cultural fit, growth potential, strategic partnership etcetera. However, in many cases, just 20% of the customers accounts for 80% of the company's profitability.

On the other side of the customer base, there is a small group of customers (again approximately 20%) who complain a lot, pay late or not at all, and only care about the price. You often do not make money on them, and these customers are mostly an energy drain for your people, since they always complain and never give any compliments. The larger part of the customer base (in many management books referred to as 'the middle 60%') consists of 'normal customers', not the big money-makers, but profitable nevertheless.

▶

Customer Segmentation

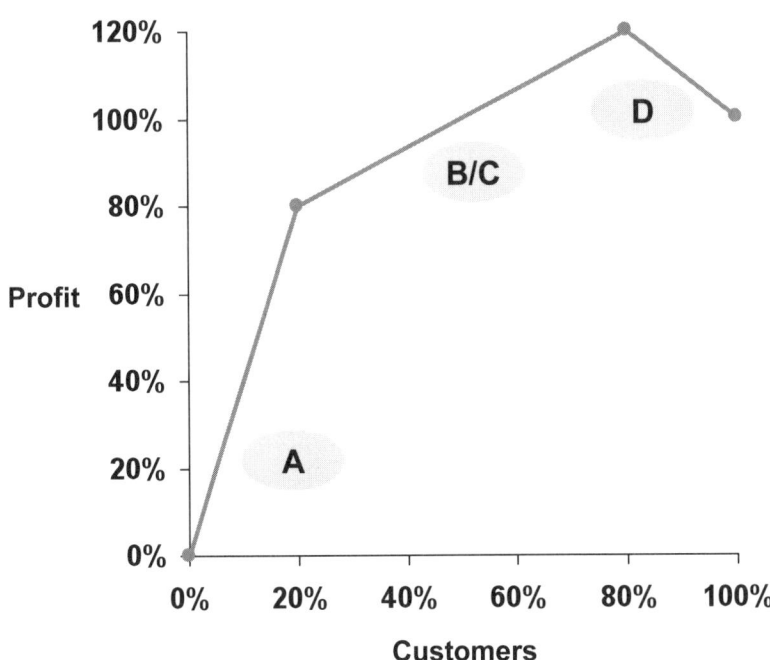

Try to involve the company's 20% most valuable customers as much as possible. We involve these customers to a high degree in fine-tuning our company's mission, in developing new products, and in any other major changes. We try to evaluate our customer base together with our customers. We label our customers A, B, C and D (see graph). 'A' customers have the highest status and are involved in almost everything we do. As such, they get top service. 'B' customers are normal customers with growth potential, while 'C' customers get the lowest level of service. 'D' customers are customers that we try to send to our biggest competitor.

Q: What percentage of your customers contributes 80% to your profitability?

"It is the dream of every leader to create an atmosphere in which all employees continuously improve themselves and the business, without interference from their superiors"

12. Deepdown, everybody wants to improve continuously

My philosophy on people's appetite for continuous improvement is quite radical. Many parents and managers might disagree with me, or even not like me for my views on this matter. In my opinion, people are born with the wish to improve themselves continuously. In many cases, people stop developing and improving themselves because their parents or their bosses have not created the right atmosphere for improvement.

Thinking back to the first years of my son's life and the many other babies around him playing and growing up, I was struck by the fact that they all showed continuous improvement. As parents, we simply encourage them, trust them and applaud them after every new step. We also comfort them and help them to try again when they fail. However, I noticed that older kids in the street were not so keen to be told what to do by their parents. All of that made me think about my role as a manager. Of course, it is the dream of every leader to create an atmosphere in which all employees continuously improve themselves and the business, without interference from their superiors.

In my team, I try to create the same atmosphere as we have at home. I want to be trustworthy, and I trust every single person working for me. I tell less and ask more. I do not want to be bossy, I want to be a facilitator and a coach - but only if people in my team want me to be their coach. I rarely tell my people what to do, or at least only as often as they tell me. This doesn't mean they can do whatever they want, but it also doesn't mean that I can do what I want. Just like at home, we set boundaries. Within these boundaries, I encourage people to keep on trying after a specific drawback, and I take time to give compliments. I admit and share personal mistakes, to show that nobody is perfect. Most importantly, I try to create an atmosphere of trust.

I do not believe colleagues who say that they have people in their teams who do not want to change, do not want to join the rest of the group in trying to beat the competition by improving themselves and the overall business continuously. Some people just lose their wish to explore and develop along the way, because they have not been supported well enough. I am confident that almost everyone can be brought back to his/her instinct to explore, develop and improve. As a leader, it is your responsibility to get your people back on board. It will make the world a better place, and it is good for business.

Q: How do you enable your people to improve themselves continuously?

Value driver model - heating company

	2001	2002	2003	2004	2005	2006	2007
Service business							
Number of contracts	39,400	37,100	35,630	35,720	37,690	39,210	40,500
Gross margin per contract	93	92	91	89	91	94	96
Contracts per FTE	510	490	485	485	550	600	700
Margin service	€ 1,733	€ 1,520	€ 1,406	€ 1,338	€ 1,717	€ 2,052	€ 2,442
Installation business							
Number of devices sold	1,150	900	920	1,050	1,300	1,350	1,400
Gross margin per device	810	790	800	820	830	835	835
Installations per FTE	41	43	39	45	47	51	53
Margin installations	€ 230	€ 188	€ 146	€ 278	€ 388	€ 465	€ 509
Others	€ 2,240	€ 2,235	€ 2,235	€ 2,900	€ 1,530	€ 1,530	€ 1,530
Profit before tax	-€ 277	-€ 527	-€ 683	-€ 1,284	€ 574	€ 987	€ 1,420

(not actual figures)

"I like to have a model (spreadsheet) which fits on to one piece of paper, representing only the five to ten key value drivers of the company"

13. Profit distribution in value driver model

Most companies I have worked with have had a difference in profitability per 'Product Market Combination' (PMC) within the company. We tend to call the overview of profit per PMC the 'profit distribution' of our company. A one-page value driver model helps me to keep an overview on where we are most and least successful.

Every company has its weak product(s) or customers. Not many companies have a book-keeping system that can control profitability per product and per customer. The dream of every controller is that every buck, euro or whatever currency comes in or out has a link to a specific product or service and a specific customer. When you then link every customer to an account manager, you can create every report and have every insight you might want to have.

The reason why many companies do not have this system in place is the administrative burden. I have never worked in a company where such a system was in place. The profit and loss structure in the companies I have worked with was mostly influenced by the way the company shows its figures to the outside world (accountants / investors). The typical format used for external reporting (turnover, cost of goods sold, gross margin, salaries, other costs, depreciations, EBIT, interest, tax, net profit) in many cases serves as the management's dashboard as well.

I do not think all companies should implement a data warehouse, where one can query and drill down in every way possible. However, I do think it is good to try to calculate the gross margin minus the direct cost per product and per market segment every once in a while. I like to do this exercise when I start in a leadership position in a new company. In the old days, I used to be an Excel wizard. I just love Excel modelling: my hobby used to be building 5MB spreadsheets, going into every single detail and having over 100 assumptions and buttons to play around with to model the effect of specific measures.

Nowadays I like to have a model (spreadsheet), which fits on to one piece of paper, representing only the five to ten key value drivers of the company. It should be modelled three years back and three years forward. For every driver, we calculate the average margin or the average cost. We only model direct costs; the indirect costs are covered in one line at the bottom of the page. This piece of paper will only partly represent reality, but it gives quite a good indication of where your company or business unit is and is not creating value.

Q: How are you currently working on the least profitable part of your business?

"My vision is that every big change within a company should be

planned and executed with the involvement of key customers"

14. Involve your key customers in major changes

Most mature companies have a strong product development process. The world is changing fast and companies have to adapt through continuous improvement of their product portfolio.

Over the years, I have asked many managing directors for their view on the 'best practice' product development process, and I have learnt that there are many different approaches that can work. However, there is one thing that almost all MD's have told me is a prerequisite for successful product development: the involvement of all internal departments of the company. This is very important (though very difficult to achieve).

In my company, we try to increase the involvement of all internal departments in two ways. The first one is the involvement of the company's managing director, or someone else who heads all departments affected by a particular change or innovation. The MD does not need to head the meeting, or to say a lot: he just needs to show his involvement. His involvement increases the willingness among attendees at the meeting to generate results.

The next level up for increasing the involvement of all internal departments is inviting key customers to join the innovation meetings. It is fantastic to see how the energy in the room changes when a customer joins the meeting. Many employees of companies do not have customer contact on a regular basis. To say it even more firmly, most people (especially in bigger companies) have never met a customer at all. The term 'common enemy' is completely the wrong word to describe what happens between the internal departments when a customer steps in, but the strong bonding effect that results is similar.

My vision is that every big change within a company should be planned and executed with the involvement of key customers. On the one hand, this helps ensure that the innovation serves market needs and strengthens the company's position against its competitors. On the other hand, it creates a bonding effect and interdepartmental alignment that may be lacking in the company.

Q: Which customer would you invite to join one of your meetings?

"Focus on customer satisfaction and employee satisfaction and you will make your shareholders happy"

15. Yearly satisfaction surveys are not effective

Focus on customer satisfaction and employee satisfaction and you will make your shareholders happy. Over the years, my company has conducted many customer surveys to test whether we were on the right track. Once a year, we would ask an external company to call a large number of our customers with a set of predefined questions. The result was a statistically robust set of insights. The results were presented to the management team and the sales and marketing team. In most cases we discussed the results for hours, looking for the reasons behind specific results. Did we ask the wrong question, did we ask it the wrong way, did we ask the wrong person or at the wrong time? It always resulted in setting up a workforce and digging further into the results of the survey, to make sure we took the correct actions and started the right internal changes to improve satisfaction. Finally, months later, we might have changed one or two aspects of our processes or behaviour. We then went on doing our thing, conducting the same test a year later.

We changed our approach after a colleague and I attended an 'MBA in a day' seminar given by a gentleman by the name of Ben Tiggelaar. Ben inspired us to stop asking external companies to do this yearly survey, asking many customers dozens of questions. Instead, we started to let a couple of our own employees (not sales people) call just ten customers and ask them only ten questions, but repeat the procedure on a monthly basis. We try to use the same questions each time, and we rotate the employees that do the survey.

This approach has helped us to bring our employees and our customers closer together. Many staff who until now have had no customer contact, now suddenly do. This makes them think about the contribution they (for instance the risk department, the II department, etcetera) make to customer satisfaction. Additionally, they bring new expertise to the process: for instance, you can be sure that your people will be much better equipped than an external company to judge whether a specific question should be skipped or another question should be added.

▶

Make sure to create a standard report on the outcome of the call, and to save the information as well, so the account manager knows what he or she needs to do. Avoid asking for feedback on individuals, but keep it general, asking, for example: "Are you happy with our service, are we easy to reach, do you like our website?" etcetera. We currently use a mixture of some open and some closed questions. I can really recommend using at least the following questions:

1. What do you really like about our company?
2. What could we have done better lately?
3. Would you recommend us?

The nice spin-off of this way of working is that it has greatly improved communication lines within the company. It's not only the salespeople who can tell what our customers think and need. In addition, the departments who normally did not have customer contact have started thinking and talking about improvements. This is one of the cornerstones of a self-steering company. It is more effective when the customer says that your company is getting too expensive for the value delivered, than when you as a manager tell your people that you want to start a cost-cutting programme, or that more quality in service and products is needed.

Dare to ask the customer for a compliment (i.e. ask them "What are we doing well?"), since working in a company purely focused on improvement, without getting compliments, is no fun. Compliments give people the energy to strive for further improvements. We have applied this approach to our employee satisfaction surveys. Every month a limited set of employees asks a limited set of questions, to a limited set of other employees. It works brilliantly.

Q: What would be the top five questions you would ask your customer?

"I start off by spending time on becoming a team, and only afterwards on attracting the customer. Making a profit should be the result of the first two steps"

16. Time management

Thinking about what you want to focus your time on is important. When you focus on visiting customers, your sales will receive a boost. When you focus on product development, the company will get more innovative, and when you focus on your employees, they will get more productive. Here, I would like to share my learning on time management.

I divide my timeslots between the following groups: employees, customers and others (including my boss or shareholders). When the business I am heading is in a stable situation, I try to spend equal time with each group. However, when I start a job in a company which is not in a stable situation (making a loss), I start off by spending time on becoming a team, and only afterwards on attracting the customer. Making a profit should be the result of the first two steps.

I spend a lot of time facilitating (i.e. coaching and mentoring) my direct reports. In addition to that, I like to have a role in the development of the top ten 'high potentials' and the top ten under-performers. Together with the manager of the employee, I decide on the role I should take in that person's development. I try to spend two hours per week on coaching and mentoring. I take a random walk for an hour a day through the office, just to chitchat. On Fridays, I invite three random employees for lunch. The subject we discuss can be football or the latest gossip, but I also use it to try out some of my thoughts on improvements within our company.

I currently work in a B2B environment, in which I focus on the top ten key accounts. Every week I visit one of them, so I see them approximately four times a year. I try to get out of a customer / supplier relationship and into a partner relationship. I also like 'top to top' meetings, where our management team meets the management team of our key customers. I like to join the sales force in winning two new business prospects with key account potential each year. Sometimes I help teams working to end relationships with business customers that are not adding value.

We created a list of our top stakeholders. On our list, we have some banks, some suppliers, universities and schools (for recruitment purposes), some media and some regulatory organisations. We work with '1', '2' or '3-star' stakeholders (a tongue-in-cheek reference to the Michelin star restaurants, where we, as a small company, of course never eat)! '1-star' means that one manager is involved, '2-star' means that a manager and someone from the management team are involved, and '3-star' means the Managing Director is involved as well.

▶

I spend the rest of my time on recurring meetings: our management team meeting (two hours every two weeks), our monthly shareholder meeting, the performance board (a monthly meeting with the senior managers), the innovation board (a monthly meeting on the top three changes in our product portfolio), a quarterly risk meeting and a company event twice a year.

I would never be able to manage my time if I would not have a top assistant to help me. The most important person in my team is my personal assistant.

STAKEHOLDER OLYMPICS

THE EMPLOYEE
THE CUSTOMER   THE MANAGER'S BOSS

Q: Do you spend your time on the things you really need to?

"If you want your organisation to keep promises, you need to keep promises yourself"

17. Keep track of actions and promises

Keeping promises increases your credibility. If you want your organisation to keep promises, you need to keep promises yourself. You ask a lot from your organisation and the organisation will only deliver if they trust you, and when you do what you have promised. Just like many managers before me, I enjoyed Stephen Covey's 'Seven Habits of Highly Effective People'.

The chapter on importance versus urgency inspired me the most. People tend to spend too much of their time doing things that are urgent but of little importance (for instance immediately answering your last voice-mail or e-mail). As a result, they tend to spend too little time on things that are not urgent but very important (like visiting prospective customers, thanking people for exceptional efforts, or having regular calls with key customers).

Wherever I go, I always carry a page of notes for myself (see graph). On one side of the paper I write down all things that are urgent, but not important. I use this side of the paper on a day-to-day, meeting-by-meeting basis. My notes are short, holding a 'who' and a 'what'. For instance: 'Nancy: Philips', reminding me to call Nancy and tell her I met one of her customers (Philips) at a seminar and promised the customer that Nancy and I would drop by for a meeting in the coming weeks.

I note these things, but I do not act immediately. Every morning when I come into the office, I spend five minutes on my one-pager to see which things have become important. I mark those issues, to make sure I act that day. When the one-pager gets too full, I update the electronic version and make a fresh print.

On the other side of the paper, I write the important but non-urgent things. I try to spend five minutes a week going through these points, to check whether I am still focusing on the right things.

▶

General:

Henno:	BP08 / mail Klaas / doc Anna / Sales speech / MT+ 3 hours
Henno:	Leon Heeze / Volta (passport) / VCA
BJ:	AvW / B2C prices
Jos:	Authorisations / Monthly report
Harry Brons:	EES (meeting Kees / Henno)
Kees:	Road show / WES / VAR issues / subsidies
Rene O:	PPA
Elze:	B2B & EMG
AdM:	PC / AOC
Anneke:	Mobile / DR's / AdM - PC / EH get to know / B2B call
Sally:	margin per m3, margin per kwh / contract
Paul:	Insurance Volta
Arjan:	EMG training
Kees v B:	Visit WES

VAR:

Pieter:	VAR calculation / RM day by day / MT EWES
Peter B:	SLA EMG - EWES

Sales:

Henno:	Illness Bert
Marcel:	Vision WES / CO2 swap
Tom:	Win rate / Mark / Communication customers / 303 - 101
Roelof:	Contracts EES in KBS / reporting / Johan Boekholt AOIC
Johan B:	AOIC

Trade / Portfolio management:

Martijn:	Sorry
Tim:	Teach Henno
Marcel:	Teach Henno

The good thing is that you do not need to act as a fire fighter, calling someone with an urgent question. You gather your notes, and when you meet the specific person, you can walk through them. It helps me to focus and stay on top of things, in control of my time, and it ensures delivery on promises. For me it has proven to be especially helpful at the start of a new job, or when things are very hectic. Just a simple one-pager, thanks for the inspiration Stephen.

Q: Would your employees say you never forget a thing?

"Senior leaders always work with three arguments, three questions or three reasons"

18. 3 is the magic number

I used to wonder why senior managers often back up their opinions using three arguments. A few years ago, a McKinsey consultant gave me an amusing explanation. He told me that in business, the number three is as important as the number seven in the holy bible. He said business is a jungle, full of people who want to gain power. If you say something, especially in a group, there will always be someone else who will try to be smarter than you are.

He told me three is the magic number for making a powerful statement. Three arguments get the least objection, independent from the content of the arguments. If you give one argument, it is easy for someone else to counter that one argument. If you give two arguments, it is easy to counter the first or the second, breaking down half of your story.

By giving three arguments, your audience gets the impression that you have given the matter considerable thought. They need time to chew on what you have just said, and they will not have had the chance or the time to start picking on one. Even if they were to pick on one, it would only reduce the power of your story by one third, which might not have much impact.

On the other hand, four arguments are too many. People get bored, you look over-prepared and people don't like that. They will just pick randomly on the last of the four arguments. Independent from the fact that it will only break down a quarter of your story, they just want to pick on you.

I am not sure if this is completely true, but I like the story. One thing is certain: senior leaders always work with three arguments, three questions, or three reasons. Something must be special about three.

Q: How often do you use three arguments to stress your

opinion?

"The three main responsibilities of a leader are to set the agenda, determine the tone of voice and nominate the senior people"

19. The three main responsibilities of a managing director

Are you a leader or a manager? Ben Verwaayen (CEO of Alcatel-Lucent) once asked me this question. He explained that: "A manager is concerned with doing things correctly and a leader is concerned with making sure the right things are done". Then he told me something I really liked, and which I still practise today. He said a leader is responsible for three things:

1. Setting the agenda
2. Determine the tone of voice
3. Nominating the senior management

The first responsibility of a leader is to set the agenda - the company's reason for being, and its main goals and targets. You do not need to develop all of these yourself, but make sure there is a process which results in your company knowing its reason for being. The closer the personal missions and goals of the employees are to the corporate mission and brand, the stronger your company will be.

You set the tone of voice. Employees look to you, and the rest of the company copies many of your behaviours. It is not possible to be an open company if you never stand in front of the troops and are open about yourself. Nor is it possible to run a cost-cutting programme when you dine in expensive restaurants all the time. If you are open about your mistakes, your people will be open about theirs. The CEO has a strong influence on the tone of voice within the company.

The team around you reflects your ambition. You need to nominate the right people to fulfil the mission and to spread the right tone of voice. Changes in your team will cost a lot of time, trust and money. Make sure you choose the right people from the start.

Q: Do you act the part of a leader or a manager?

IT'S HARD WORK BRINGING STAKEHOLDERS TOGETHER

"The leader is the central person, connecting and trying to align all stakeholders"

20. Stakeholder alignment

As a manager, you may well be the central point of all your company's stakeholders. You are responsible for making all your stakeholders happy - your boss, your shareholders, your employees and your customers. Unfortunately, they may not have the same views on all subjects. By trying to make all of them happy, you may often find yourself representing each of them towards the others. Here are some examples:

Representing the employees towards the shareholders: "Dear shareholder, based on this salary benchmark, we think that increasing employee salaries is fair".

Representing the shareholders towards the employee: "Dear employees, looking at this benchmark of the returns in our sector, we are under-performing".

Representing the customers towards the employees: "Dear employee, our competitors are delivering higher quality at lower prices, we're losing customers, so we need to cut costs".

The Managing Director is the central person, connecting and trying to align all the company's stakeholders. I have learnt that this job is much easier when you bring your stakeholders together in person, instead of being the mail carrier, trying to align them by running around from one to the other. Here I will give some examples of how I try to be less of a mail carrier and more of an orchestrator, aligning stakeholders:

1. involve your key customers in major changes in your company;
2. set regular meetings between your management team and your key accounts;
3. test your mission in a joint meeting with representatives of your key stakeholders.

It takes courage to bring stakeholders together. You will have to be more open than you are used to being. You might feel like you are losing power, since your role as the representative of one group towards the other disappears.

However, the funny thing is that the more I focused on bringing stakeholders together physically, the more successful we became as a company.

Q: Do you feel resistance to bringing stakeholders together in person? If so, why?

"People will be fonder of an idea if you say someone else had it"

21. It wasn't my idea

Some years ago, I did a little experiment for how to sell an idea. I had an idea on a specific marketing campaign that I thought would fit to the new direction we were taking as a company. To test the idea, I talked to approximately twenty people: some employees; some customers; some shareholder representatives and some externals.

I played a bit with the way I presented my idea. Half of the time, I said I had had a great idea, then explained it. The other half of the time, I said someone else had had a great idea. Depending on who I talked to, I said the idea was from a customer or an employee or a shareholder etcetera.

It might have been a coincidence, or it might say something about my image in those days :-), but people were fonder of the idea if I said someone else had had it than if I said it was my own idea. I think there is a more level playing field between you and the person you discuss the idea with when neither of you has had the idea. Total ownership of it leaves the other person no space to explore with you on common ground.

I also noticed that if my counterpart did not like the idea, it was much easier for me to defend that idea, since I was not as emotionally involved. This was a very interesting lesson for me on the importance of ego and emotion in convincing others.

Q: To which person would you present your idea as someone else's?

"Use energy from other people to energise your team"

22. Fire up your team

The dream of every manager is to work with a highly creative, productive team, with a high level of ownership, in an atmosphere of trust, in which people are open and have fun. These are the teams that improve themselves and their organisation continuously. I strongly believe that a manager can create these teams. It may be a naïve belief, but I have had it since the first time I was allowed to head a team, and so far it has worked. Sometimes it takes a little time, sometimes a long time, but it is possible.

Apart from using your own energy and skills to fire up your team, you might try to think about other ways to get a constructive discussion going, by inviting other people to your team sessions. Here I will give some examples of how one might use energy from other people to fire up (energise) your own team.

Suggestions:
1. Invite someone who does your job in a different company or another branch to share insights with you and your team;
2. Ask a key customer to join a team meeting to discuss his/her perception of your team or company;
3. Read this book together, and discuss one column per week :-)

Q: Who would you ask to help you fire up your team?

23

"I make every investment decision as if it were my own money"

23. Would you invest your own money?

A couple of years ago, I had to make a difficult business decision on whether or not to make a large investment. I could not get my head around all the pros and cons. My boss suggested I forget everyone elses' opinions and asked me if I would invest in the project myself. That helped – it gave me a clear view on what to do.

Since then I make every investment decision as if it were my own money. Would I take this risk with my own cash? Would I postpone this action until next year? What would I change first thing in the morning if this company belonged to me? Would I put my own equity in this development? I ask these questions a lot to myself and to my team.

In bigger companies, many senior people are involved in deciding whether someone is ready to go to the next level within the company. Since I have always been very fond of progressing to the next level, I once tried to please some senior people by working on a strategy that I did not agree with. Because I simply didn't believe in what I was doing, I did not work passionately on the project. I would never have invested my own money in the strategy we were following. The project turned out to be not successful. I took part of the blame and did not make it to the next level that year.

I have become a much more effective operator since I decided to focus only on investments that I would be prepared to put my own money into. It takes some courage to stand tall and say no to projects you do not believe in. Obviously, you cannot say no too often if you want to stay in a specific department or company. However, I have learnt that it is better to switch jobs when your job does not feel right than to collaborate on things that just do not feel good, and on which you would not spend your own money. Part of being successful is to trust your intuition.

Q: What would you change if the company you work for were yours?

"A consistent method for staff evaluation is important,

especially with a new team"

24. Staff evaluation methodology

One of the most interesting yearly management team (MT) meetings is the one in which we try to get a common view on the performance and the potential of our workforce. Our Human Resources (HR) manager chairs this meeting. We have learnt that taking sufficient time to discuss the definition of the different levels of potential and performance is very important.

We rank both performance and potential. The question is how to make this ranking exercise objective. To our opinion, it will never be 100% objective - we can only try to make it as objective as possible. Discussing every score on every employee is a way to do this. Here I list some of the questions that have helped us to evaluate our staff in a consistent matter:

1. What is the goal of ranking our workforce?
2. Which programmes will we offer our 'high potentials' and our under-performers?
3. Do we benchmark people against each other or only against their own targets?
4. Should we adjust for market circumstances?
5. Can someone be a high performer when he/she does not care about our values?

A consistent method for staff evaluation is important, particularly for a new team. We like to do a dry run a couple of months before the real ranking needs to be done, to be sure there is a common understanding of the system we use. We openly discuss the fact that it is easier to tell someone he is over-performing than to tell him he is under-performing. We also discuss the fact that it is tempting for any of us to try to keep the best people in our own teams.

Visualising the results of the ranking for smaller groups by plotting all staff members in a performance / potential matrix helps to increase consistency (see graph).

Many multinationals - at least the ones I have worked for - run the process of ranking before yearend, at a time when it is not yet clear whether targets have been reached. I do not really understand this, since it does not help to make the ranking objective. However, we now work around this by using latest estimates instead of real performance indicators.

▶

To increase objectivity, we ask our controlling team to prepare a latest estimate versus budget of the key performance indicators. The first check we do, as a team, is to see whether the targets and performance of the company are in line. After that, we do the same for each department. These are interesting benchmarks in defining performance per employee.

We have learnt that team leaders do not like to lose their best team members, since it might endanger their team's performance. A rule we like a lot is the following: a manager can only become a 'high potential' if he promotes his best performing team member to a higher job outside of his own team at least once every three years.

Employees: Performance and Potential

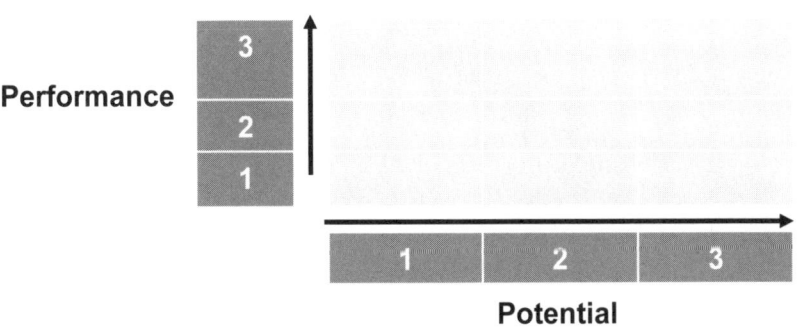

Q: Does your ranking process improve the performance of your company?

"If you want your people to stay motivated, you have to react fast"

25. React fast

You determine the swiftness of your troops. I try to react to every email I receive within 24 hours. If you want your people to stay motivated, you have to react fast. Nothing kills initiative more than having to wait for an answer from senior management.

When I was a young manager, I thought I was improving the company's performance by checking all proposals and new ideas in depth, sometimes coming up with long lists of corrections. When I did not have time to do an in-depth check of the contents of a proposal, it sometimes took me days to get back to someone. In doing so, I slowed the process down and killed the feeling of ownership.

Nowadays, I always try to react within 24 hours, giving a maximum of 2-3 tips on how content might be improved. I leave it open to people whether or not they follow my advice. In this way, the level of ownership increases, and hence the quality of content. The speed of our projects has increased and so has our overall performance.

Q: How many emails lie in your inbox unanswered for more than 24 hours?

"A drawback will make you stronger if you don't take it too personally"

26. Don't be scared of drawbacks

One of my first bosses used to say: "Always save some energy for the last surprise". Life is full of surprises and you cannot influence everything. There always is the 'luck' factor that affects whether or not you reach your goals.

When watching my son and some other kids learning to walk, I noticed that not every child has the same predefined talents and not every child tries as hard as the rest. Talent and persistence determine performance, but you still need luck to be successful. In those days, I invented the following formula:

$$SUCCESS = PERFORMANCE \times LUCK$$

The more luck you have, the less persistent you need to be, and vice versa. The better you know your own strengths and weaknesses, the easier it will be to choose a direction in life, where the chances of success are fair. However, drawbacks will occur - they're just a part of life. And just like with sports, your form is not only determined by the length of time you are able to exercise and by your speed or power, but also by the time you need to recover. The time you need to be ready for the next race.

Before I reached my 30's, I was mostly concerned about avoiding drawbacks in business life. Then I met someone who helped me find a way to speed up the time it took me to recover from drawbacks. The better I got at recovering from drawbacks, the more I was able to explore. A drawback will make you stronger if you don't take it too personally, but personally enough to learn your lesson and not to blame the rest of the world.

Q: What was the difference in your reaction between your latest drawback and your first?

"My intuition protested but I carried on... Big mistake"

27. Listen to your intuition

There is an old Dutch saying that goes: "Trust comes by foot but leaves by horse". It takes a long time to gain people's trust, but your trustworthiness can be lost in a second. Intuition is a fantastic thing. On a recent occasion I did not follow my intuition, and this almost cost me the trust of some important people.

The headquarters (HQ) were preparing our company for the expected danger of the H1N1 flu. They asked all senior managers to list their 'non-expendable' employees. I wanted to answer that none of our employees are 'expendable', knowing that that would not be the answer HQ was expecting, but although my intuition protested, I carried on and listed some people. Big mistake!

Two weeks later, the HQ asked one of the employees in my unit whether all our non-expendable employees were able to work at home in case the office became a no-go area due to the virus. Unfortunately this question was asked to someone in my unit who, like me, also did not listen to her intuition. She wrote to all non-expendable people, saying:

"Dear colleague, you have been ear-marked by the Managing Director as non-expendable. We are currently making sure the company keeps on going when the flu kicks in, and I would therefore like to know whether you are able to work at home. Please indicate availability of printer, web connection, etc."

My goodness, within minutes, the e-mail got forwarded all around the company, and within half an hour I had the first employee at my desk, wanting to know why I thought he was expendable. What could I do? A terrible situation. I had been working on being trustworthy, open and transparent for such a long time and now this.

I decided to send an e-mail to all those on the 'non-expendable' list, telling them I had made a big mistake in following a corporate initiative that did not feel right in the first place. I said that we would not follow this approach and that all employees would be treated equally when push came to shove.

Q: When was the last time you did not listen to your intuition? Do you still regret it?

28

"Try to put new employees into pole position"

28. Introduction programmes

Getting a good start is key to winning a race. Try to put new employees in pole position.

When I started my first job (a big bank in Brussels, Belgium), they showed me a chair, a desk, a computer, a telephone and a cupboard. I was instructed that I needed to clean out the cupboard myself and left to my own devices. Two years later, I joined an introduction programme to get to know the bank. Too late! The bank missed the chance to get me in the right modus from the start.

In my current company we put a great deal of effort into organising introduction days for new staff. On these days, the Managing Director welcomes all new employees, and makes sure they feel needed and at home. During the day, the new people get acquainted with the mission, vision and strategy of our company, the market (we invite a customer), the shareholders, the values of the company, recent successes and current issues. We present our talent and training programmes and the way we do evaluations, and we emphasise the importance of increasing employee and customer satisfaction.

At the end of the day, we do something nice, such as sending the new employees home with a gadget, a nice briefcase or similar, giving them the feeling that they did not just join a company, but a family. A family on a mission, in which they are more needed than anybody else in the world.

When people start working, they will (mostly) not be effective and efficient as of day one, so why not give them time to learn? Set up a small, informal introduction programme, in which the first month will serve as a tour through the company. Include in the tour places like the customer contact centre (so the new people can experience real customer contact) and the controlling department (so they can see whether the company is making the shareholders happy). You might even think of setting up an exchange programme with some of your key customers, exchanging employees for a day or a week.

Someone once told me to ask new people to share their first experiences after their first month. I really like doing so, since new people still have a fresh perspective on the business.

Q: How long do you think it should take before a new employee feels at home?

"It's not only about what you say in a meeting, but also about how, to whom and when"

29. Step on the brakes to go faster

After a few years in the working world, I found I was not very happy. I come from a very warm-hearted, open family and during my school and university years, I only hung out with people I liked. Suddenly I had to work with a group of people, some of whom I would not naturally have chosen to work with. I started with a very positive "okay let's conquer the world" feeling and tried to turn the team into the same open environment which I knew from the old days - that is, open, constructive feedback and results-orientated, combined with lots of fun.

After a couple of years, I knew something was wrong. I could not get my message across in team meetings. Too many people weren't interested in my opinion or even started to talk behind my back. For some reason, I was not the only one who felt bad in the team, and our manager decided we should work with a coach for a day or two. For me this session was a totally new world. Suddenly all the topics that I wanted to talk about were on the table. I did not care if they were positive or negative for me, it just felt good to talk about them. I loved the openness and the honesty we reached at the end of the session, sharing our dreams and giving each other compliments and tips for improvement.

The first weeks after the session were fine, but then the atmosphere in the team deteriorated again. We hadn't learnt a thing. I was part of a team that was not able to coach itself. I did my best to go on being open and honest, giving feedback to everyone, and trying to combine a tip with a compliment. However, the team did not appreciate my behaviour. I talked to my manager about it and he allowed me to join a management development programme, with the specific task of finding out why I did not feel good.

The programme had a couple of different elements to it, of which I liked the personal development part the most. During this part of the programme, we had to describe where we came from, where we stood now and where we wanted to be in three years' time. Divided over three sessions, I had deep discussions with my coach (Frans), who later became a good friend. Frans taught me that it's not only about what you say in a meeting, but also about how, to whom and when.

▶

Together with Frans, we created a mantra stating: "Step on the brakes to go faster" - meaning I should take a moment (step on the brake) before I said something in a meeting. In that moment, I had to decide whether I should say it in the meeting or after the meeting in a one-to-one. What a relief. That is what had kept me from feeling good. Stepping on the brakes really made me go faster. Before that, too many people felt offended by my feedback, tips and ideas. After the meeting, in one-to-ones, my colleagues appreciated my open and honest feedback.

Years later, I found out that the manager of a team has great impact on how open a team can be. I even doubt whether a team needs a coach when a manager is able to create an open environment.

Q: Did you ever need a coach in teams where there was already a high level of trust?

ZZZZ ZZZZ ZZZZ

30

"Making people feel at home in the office is a way to show trust in your workforce"

30. Inspiring location, inspiring people

The look and feel of an office is an important part of a company's identity. I believe people tend to adapt to the environment in which they work. Since more and more people work in offices, the need for some kind of identity within these buildings is increasing. Many office buildings look the same from the inside. You see desks, computers, printers, a coffee machine, dying plants and some art of which nobody knows who bought it and why.

Interior designers for office buildings recognise the need for change, and many developments are under way in this area, such as open offices, meeting boxes and full flex chairs and desks. Changes in the working environment do not need to be costly. A fresh look is important, as well as some leisure space. In my company, we changed a meeting room into a lounge room, with a boxing ball to help people get rid of some aggression. You might also think of adding a ping-pong table, table-football or a big television to watch important sport events or breaking news.

Making people feel at home in the office is another way to show trust in your workforce. It is about performance, not about the number of hours people are in the office. Industrial times are over.

We once had a painting workshop with some teams, where we chose the best paint colour for our office walls. This gave a homely feeling, which is quite appropriate, since many of us spend more time awake in the office than awake at home. On the other hand, people working in non-inspiring interiors might spend more time sleeping in the office than they are sleeping at home :-)

Q: Who would you ask to come up with a plan to spice up the office interior?

31

"Keeping a diary is perfect preparation for staff evaluation meetings"

31. Keep a diary

Intuition is a very important source for evaluating competences and behaviour of staff. My intuition often tells me whether someone has performed well or not. Many events from before the period of evaluation will have influenced my intuition, but this does not help me to get my opinion across to the employee I am evaluating. I often struggle to remember the occasions that have strongly affected my opinion, and for this reason, I keep a small diary.

Once a month, I take 30 minutes to update a one-pager, on which I write down compliments and tips for all my direct reports. Sometimes there is nothing to write for a specific person, sometimes there is. Sometimes it is something I already shared. Sometimes it is something I still need to share. I try to stay away from bringing up surprises during evaluations.

Updating the list is a nice sanity check for me, to see whether I have shared everything yet. It is also perfect preparation for the evaluation meetings. I do not like to spend several evenings writing evaluation reports, just because I can't remember any good examples to make sure we have the right discussion. Trusting on intuition alone will not help you finding the right examples to get the message across. Your statement will have little impact.

Q: How do you prepare for evaluations of your staff?

"Good inter-company charging should always be done at market prices"

32. Portfolio optimisation

I was once Chief Financial Officer of a holding company which managed a portfolio of companies. The portfolio comprised approximately twenty companies, with a broad range of activities. The companies were all small or medium-sized enterprises, running break-even or with small profits or losses. The companies had many inter-company transactions. The holding company was a small group of people, asked to optimise the portfolio.

To do so, the CEO (Toon van Kleef) and I came up with 'The three-step approach'. Not a very creative name, but it did what it had to do, bringing the message across that something important was happening and that changes were to be expected. We formed project groups for each company and worked through the following questions, in the following sequence:

1. What is the bottom-line effect on the P&L of the total multinational?
2. Is it possible to improve and grow the business?
3. Do we want to improve and grow the business, or should we spin it off?

Step one: Determining the bottom-line effect. What would be the effect on the profit of the total multinational if we did not have this company in our portfolio? In a big multinational, with many inter-company relationships, this question is very relevant, and sometimes very complex. Good inter-company charging should always be done at market prices, but it does not make sense to benchmark all intercompany charges too often. However, you need to do that when you're thinking about divesting. We benchmarked all inter-company cash flows against market prices. To give an example: we had a company in our portfolio that employed many copywriters. Twenty per cent of the company's turnover was made outside of the multinational, while all the rest was internal business. We benchmarked the company's internal fees against the fees of some of the best copywriters in the market, and we found out that market prices were much lower than the company's internal prices.

The company, which we thought was making profit (looking at the annual report) and thus adding value to the bottom line of the multinational, was actually a burden for the multinational. We substituted the internal fees for the external fees in our model, to represent the real situation, a loss-making company.

We also had a company selling security systems. We found out that the cost of some internal services was too low. In that case, we learnt that we were actually looking at a profit-making company instead of a loss making company.

▶

Step two: is it possible to improve and grow the business? Working in the same project teams, we put together improvement plans for each company. This took the largest part of the time but was the most fun. Most of the companies were not familiar with a structured improvement approach. Some of them were not interested in participating, but for most of the companies, we succeeded in creating a positive, constructive and open atmosphere. We worked very hard with a range of different teams and wrote five-year plans for most of the companies.

Step three: we calculated three values (see graph):
1. the Net Present Value (NPV) of the improvement plan (the 'grow' option);
2. the price we expected to get if we divested the business (the 'sell' option); and
3. the costs we would incur in closing the business down (the 'stop' option).

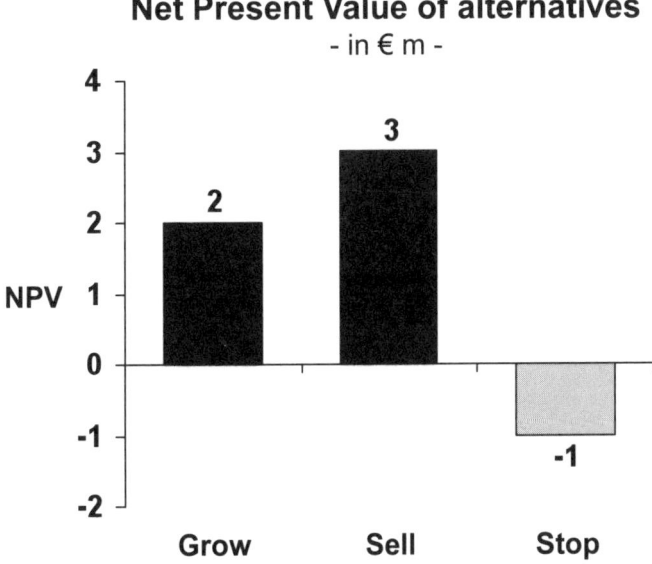

This resulted in some spin-offs, some internal mergers, and one company closing down. For the rest, we started implementing the improvement plans. The same approach works for a product portfolio. The whole exercise took us two years.

Q: Are you sure all your activities are adding value to your bottom line?

"A leader has to earn the right to lead"

33. Nightmare

What are the options of the board of a football club when the football players do not want to work with the trainer / coach anymore? My most complicated moment as a manager so far was the moment in which the team of one of my direct reports came to me to say they wanted a different manager.

It was nine o'clock in the morning when seven colleagues stepped into my office - a whole department, except their manager (the person reporting to me). Alarm bells started ringing. In a split second, I scrolled through all management books I had read. What should I do - throw them out, listen to them, ask them to come back with their manager? We sat down and before we started the conversation, I asked them: "Are you sure about the consequences this conversation might have? I don't want you to tell me anything that you haven't told your manager at least twice".

After listening to the team explain why they wanted a new manager, I asked them to come back the next day, so I could think about the situation. After consulting some other colleagues, I sat together with the team again, only this time together with the team manager and our HR manager. The team did not like the idea at first, but we had the meeting anyway. After an hour, we were sure that we were not able to solve the situation at the table and I asked whether the team would be willing to take two weeks to have some individual and some group sessions with a mediator. Two weeks later, the team informed me that they could not solve the problem. I had to make a decision.

▶

I was in a bit of a dilemma: on the one hand, I had the feeling that the team should have given the manager more time to find the right way of leading the team. On the other hand, the manager lacked some crucial competencies to lead this team. The company as a whole was suffering badly from the crisis within this specific department. I had to act and I decided to try to find a way to take a measure that would affect the whole group (both the manager and the team).

What we did was the following: we terminated all temporary contracts (the manager was one of the people with a temporary contract) and shifted some people (incl. their responsibilities) to other departments, leaving only a very small group of people. I asked the remaining people in the department to take four weeks to work out a plan for the way forward for the department. I appointed a project leader (someone who was not part of the department, who I thought might eventually become the new manager). An important part of the project was a range of satisfaction interviews with the customers of the department.

After four weeks, during which the team had some very confronting interviews, the team drew the conclusion that it was time for a big change. I appointed the project leader to become the boss of the team and approved all proposed changes. I allowed the new manager to fill the temporary contracts with new people. I had some individual talks to the old employees still in the department, telling them I supported the new manager, whatever happened. My message was VERY clear.

This situation showed me once again that a leader has to earn the right to lead. I still feel bad for the contracts we terminated, but after almost a year, the department became one of the best-performing departments in our company.

Q: What would you do if a team did not accept its leader?

34

"Setting up a think tank solved our issue of having no time for projects"

34. Think tank

A year ago, my company established a think tank group (or special projects team). I can highly recommend creating a similar forum if you are running a company of at least 100 employees. Our think tank comprises just two employees, these are people who like to be where the action is.

We created this group to conduct projects all over the company. The department does not have a specific task, nor does it have specific targets. They do projects for different departments, and based on project evaluations, the think tank evaluates itself.

We realised that we had not been working on many strategic topics, due to a focus on operational issues. We had neglected things like setting up a customer survey, redefining a department's mission, and orchestrating the strategic planning process.

Setting up a think tank has solved our issue of having no time for projects. It has increased the number and the speed of successful projects. Furthermore, has it lowered our out-of-pocket costs, since we work less with consultants. It also keeps competitive know-how within our company. However, responsibility for continuous improvement, the company's strategic direction and the result of the projects remains with the departmental managers, not with the think tank.

Becoming part of the think tank is an honour. We like to keep the period spent by staff members in the team short, so that many of them can gain experience in the strategic issues of other departments. This broadens peoples' horizons. It increases the level of involvement with our company and the level of interaction between departments.

Q: How much knowledge do you externalise by hiring consultants?

"I see no difference in the basic rules that apply for maintaining a private or a business relationship"

35. Relationships

Good business is built on good relationships. Good business relies on good relationships with customers, employees, suppliers, senior management and many other stakeholders. And good relationships are very important for a company and its employees if they want to be effective, successful and happy.

The other day I was wondering if there is any difference between a private relationship and a business relationship, or between the relationship with a supplier and with a customer. Someone once told me that one has to be professional at work and that you can be yourself at home. One should always please the customer and squeeze the supplier. I do not agree.

I see no difference in the basic rules that apply for maintaining a private or a business relationship. Neither do I see an advantage in maintaining a different relationship with a customer or a supplier, with my boss or with an employee. It is always about balancing between what you get for what you give.

DARLING, YOU **MUST** STOP BRINGING YOUR WORK HOME!

Most people like you to listen carefully, to be honest and to say when something does not feel right. People like to develop themselves, and in good relationships, people develop in the same direction. People want to be trusted and occasionally surprised in a positive way. People do not like others to talk about them behind their back. I have learnt that when you walk away from a difficult topic it will always come back at you like a boomerang, independently from what kind of relationship you have.

Q: Do you think business relationships differ strongly from

private relationships?

"The most effective people are those that can be themselves in all situations"

36. Authenticity

There are many different forms of effective leadership. However, the most effective people are those that can be themselves in all situations. People always notice
when you are playing a role, and trying to do so can sap your energy. Being the
same person everywhere will make life easier. If you don't need to think about which
role you should be playing, you will be able to act much faster.

Obviously, it helps a lot if you find a job that fits your character, passion and dreams.
The better the job fits your character, the more effective being yourself will be. It
takes some people a long time to find the job that fits. It took me many years to find
out what I wanted - what my dream and my passion were, and which job would
allow me to be most effective and successful, just by being me.

When I was ten years old, I had a classmate called Fred. He wanted to become a
truck driver. He loved big cars, the noise of the engine and the adventure of being
on his own for days. By the time I went to university, Fred was already driving his
truck. He still is, and he still loves what he is doing.

When I was young, I dreamed of becoming either a writer or a rock star. I like to
observe and I like to entertain. For a long time, I kept this to myself, since I thought
it did not fit the business world. Nowadays I think that showing true interest (obser-
ving), making other people laugh, having a great time together, being able to get a
message across, interconnecting and winning peoples' hearts are the drivers that
make me the manager that I am.

Finding out who you really are, and what your personal 'brand' is, is a prerequisite
to being authentic. And finding the right company and the right kind of business
that best fits your personal brand will allow you to be successful, just by being
yourself.

Q: What was your dream back at school?

"I like to determine the company's mission with some of its key stakeholders"

37. The company's agenda

A managing director is responsible for setting a company's reason for being, its broad agenda; its positioning statement. As a manager, you are responsible for determining the mission for your department, and for making sure you add value to the overall agenda of the company. As an employee, you will be most effective if your personal mission fits with the environment you are working in. The most successful companies are those where the personal mission and brand of the employees fits the corporate mission and brand.

I like to determine a company's mission and agenda together with some of its key stakeholders. We never add quantities like market share or return on equity to our mission statement. We try to establish the mission in such a way that all stakeholders (customers, employees, shareholders) understand the company's reason for being. We define success in separate sessions. Customer satisfaction differs from the indicators we use for employee satisfaction, which again differ from the indicators we agree on with the shareholders. These are no secret agreements - they are just not part of our mission. I always try to establish the company's agenda.

Obviously, I have never been able to beat Kennedy's mission: "We will bring a man to the moon and back within ten years from now". However, for me this still is one of the best examples of a strong mission statement. It holds the who, the what and the when, all in one sentence.

Q: What is your company's reason for being (one

sentence)?

"I couldn't stop thinking about work... I couldn't find the off button in my head..."

38. ctrl-alt-delete

Ctrl-alt-delete is a metaphor for shutting down. A few years ago, I was having sleeping problems, as I was not able to shut down from work. My mind kept on going thinking about it late into the night. I mostly woke up around 2 or 3 am, lay awake for a couple of hours thinking about work and then would fall asleep again shortly before my alarm went off. Although I had some fine ideas overnight, I was extremely tired during the day, feeling far from sharp. I was mostly even too tired to implement the ideas I had overnight.

A little 'aside'… I still have good memories of some investment bankers I worked with on some Merger & Acquisition (M&A) deals. After a full night of modelling and number crunching, these guys were able to convincingly react "never felt better" or "like a million bucks", to my question of how they felt this morning. Ha ha ha, funny people these specialists, very tough on themselves.

But back to my sleeping problems and how I tried to cope with them... In those days, I was travelling a lot. This made me decide not to do a team sport. When I commit myself to a team, I want to be a reliable team member. Due to the travelling, I wasn't able to plan too well, so I did some sports on my own. I ran, swum and sometimes cycled. I tried to do two hours of sport a week, but even in the weeks when I managed this, I still didn't sleep well. I couldn't find the off button in my head - I just couldn't stop thinking about work. The only ctrl-alt-delete moment I had on a regular basis was an unhealthy one - Friday night beers with some of my friends. Fantastic evenings, but having a couple of beers too many was not the way I wanted to relax during the week.

▶

SWITCH OFF FROM WORK
AND KNOCK YOURSELF OUT!

After a while, I went to my doctor and explained the situation. He asked me what kind of sports I was doing and then he laughed. He told me I was doing sports which let me use my brain for things other than the exercise. He told me I was doing 'structure your thoughts' sports, which is very good, but I should combine it with 'ctrl-alt-delete' sports.

I gave him a pretty blank look, so he proceeded: "Take tennis, for instance: in tennis, you constantly need your brain to perform well. Suppose the ball is coming to your right, well then you might have to step right, but do you need one or two steps? You need to think about that, then you need to lift your arm, and the question is how high, etc... It's not possible to think about anything other than the game you're playing". This kind man taught me an interesting lesson that really helped me to relax. Since then I have slept much better.

Q: What would be your ctrl-alt-delete sport?

"The results I have achieved through trusting others are countless"

39. Trust

The world is changing faster every day, and as a result, the value of long years of business experience is decreasing. In the old days, an experienced leader could lead a company to success by managing from the top down. Nowadays, quite the opposite is true. Companies now need every single brain to be successful – it's a case of all hands on deck!

People make the difference, and in companies, success is gained through the willingness of the people within the company to improve continuously and to cope with change on a day-by-day basis. Winning companies are companies whose people drive change. Instead of initiating change top-down, the leader should create an environment in which change and continuous improvement become part of the DNA of the company. It should be an environment where people get the freedom to do what they think should be done, and where they start acting as if it is their own company.

To do so, you need to have a high level of trust in the people you work with, but trust is not easily gained. I once attended a seminar where the speaker asked the group: "Who do you trust?" It was very quiet in the room, until someone finally said: "I trust Nelson Mandela". Then someone else said, "I trust my wife and my family" and then someone said, "I trust my best friends". I said: "I trust everybody".

The whole group looked at me like I was crazy. Driving home, I couldn't stop thinking about the situation. In my view, there are two kinds of people when it comes to trust: the people who trust everybody until that trust is broken, and the people who trust nobody until they have proven they can be trusted. I initially trust everybody and can count on one hand the number of times where my trust has been broken. However, the results I have achieved through trusting others are countless.

Q: Do you have an example of a successful relationship where there was no trust?

"A successful life is a life where someone has lived his or her dream"

40. Life is short

When I listen to employees who say: "I'm doing it all for the company", I get a bit uncomfortable. I prefer people who do their thing completely for themselves. This might sound strange, but what I mean is that a successful company is a company where the mission of the company or the department fits the personal mission of the people working for that company. Those people are the company. When some-one is doing it all for the company, I cannot stop myself from asking: "That's really nice, but what do you want in life"? A successful life is a life where someone lived his or her dream.

Defining your personal mission, your dream, is one of the hardest things there is in life (at least, it was for me). I doubt whether it is possible to establish your mission at an early stage. I even doubt whether it should stay the same throughout your life. I could imagine the chance of success is higher when it stays stable, since you have more time to live your dream. On the other hand, I know many very interes-ting people who have a different dream every year. And what is success? Different for each person I guess. For me success is happiness.

Life is relatively short. If you are lucky, you get eighty years. Thinking about that helps me to make sure I do the things I want to do. My private mission is to make my family happy, read good books, go to concerts, meet friends and help people to be successful in their business life. My business mission is to improve companies by energising the people within the company, with a high level of independence for the people that I work with and a high level of independence for me. Sharing dreams and ambitions is important to be successful as a team.

Q: Do you know the dreams of your team?

"Having a good team discussion on the meaning of a particular corporate value can be more important than the value itself"

41. Values

Most likely, your company will already have determined its corporate values - usually three to four values that govern the way the company operates. The corporate values of the different companies I have worked for did not really differ much. They were mostly values like openness, respect, inspiring people, honesty or being results-driven. I never saw a corporate value of which someone might say: "Such nonsense, I don't want to be like that". The value selection process is often done in the right way, that is, bottom-up, through a carefully orchestrated and timely process. However, I have experienced in many cases that the implementation of these values leaves room for improvement.

The implementation of corporate values is not achieved simply by stating: "These are the (new) corporate values, which we will adapt in our daily work".

Corporate values are a great help for teams to have a discussion on individual interpretation, for instance, of the word 'openness'. Does it mean you have to talk a lot, that you are always honest, or that you give feedback, even when it hasn't been requested? Does it mean that you have no secrets, that you are highly transparent, or that the manager always shares information, again even when unsolicited? Having a good team discussion on the meaning of a particular corporate value can be more important than the value itself.

Discussing the values also helps teams to get to know each other better. In my company, it has helped us to confront each other with things that might not other-wise have been said. For example: "Hey Henno, I thought we agreed to be open. Didn't that mean that we're also supposed to share important information pro-actively? Why did you not tell us this or that yesterday?"

Q: What is your team's interpretation of the company's corporate values?

"During a takeover... when people from the two companies meet, it's like a cat meeting a dog"

42. Integrating companies

Over the last decade, I have been involved in many post-merger integration processes. When the multinational I worked for used to acquire a company, I was the
first one sent out to "lift the synergies". I lived temporarily in Hamburg, Hannover,
Berlin, Leipzig, Düsseldorf, Den Bosch and The Hague to be close to the company
just acquired. Two different countries, seven different cities, seven different
corporate cultures, but always the same situation; people who were uncomfortable
with the fact that their company had a new shareholder.

I do not want to mention how the new colleagues reacted to the new way of
reporting. I also do not want to mention their reactions when asked to adapt to the
corporate values of the multinational to which they now belonged. I especially don't
want to mention their reactions to the corporate risk manuals, the crisis manuals,
the audits, the accountants and the satisfaction surveys. Nor do I want to mention
their reactions to corporate procurement, legal, tax and treasury, or to the company
car policies or the new salary and bonus formats.

What I would like to mention is a specific pattern I noticed, between a company
that is taking over and a company that has been taken over. The company taking
over is mostly bigger, let's call it Big C and the smaller company small c. The main
difference between a bigger and a smaller company is that the bigger company has
a higher percentage of specialists and the smaller company has higher percentage
generalists. In other words, smaller companies have many people who understand
the whole value chain and bigger companies have many people who understand a
specific part of the value chain very well.

▶

So when people from Big C and small c meet, it's like a cat meeting a dog. When one puts up its tail, the other animal always misinterprets this (a dog puts up his tail when it is happy, a cat when it is angry). Example: Bob has been working for Big C for years, in the procurement department. He decides to pay a visit to small c, which was recently bought by Big C. Both companies are active in the same field. Bob meets Caroline from small c on a sunny Tuesday afternoon.

"Hello Caroline, nice to meet you, my name is Bob. I'm from Big C's corporate procurement department. I'm responsible for long term contracts. How is procurement arranged in your office?". Caroline replies that procurement is just one of her eight responsibilities, and admits she feels a little insecure about all the in-depth knowledge that Bob has on procurement.

Caroline is interested to know why Big C reacted in a completely different way than small c on a very important and recent change in the market. Bob starts to feel uncomfortable as well now, since he suddenly realises he doesn't have a clue about the market proposition of his company, nor does he know how the competition is doing. He only knows that he procures better than the competition.

Voila, here we have a rather uncomfortable situation, in which both try to get the conversation on a level where they feel comfortable, and where they have know-how. Unfortunately, that behaviour makes the other person even more uncomfortable, and so on and so forth. A dog talking to a cat. It can be really tough in the beginning.

What I see within our company, and within many other companies as well, is that people from Big C are sent to small c, shortly after takeover. Unfortunately it almost never happens, that people from small c are sent to Big C. That way, Big C would create ambassadors amongst small c employees.

Sending small c employees to Big C will speed up the integration process.

Q: How do you stimulate smooth co-operation after a takeover?

"Vulnerability demonstrates to your team that you are open to learn"

43. Vulnerability

Should a leader always be tough or sometimes be a little bit vulnerable as well? In my opinion, a good leader should be able to be both. Being tough is a stereotype for leaders that I have experienced very often. However, being vulnerable is often more difficult than being tough. Vulnerability demonstrates to your team that you are open to learn. If you are not open to improving yourself continuously, it will be hard to ask your people to do the same.

One of the ways to show that I am willing to learn is the way in which I like to discuss things that have gone wrong within the company. I always try to make myself part of the learning process by stating what I could have done better in a specific situation.

For instance, we once lost an important account. When I talked to my sales manager, I told him that I regretted not having spent more time with the teams outside. Some of the sales guys had asked me to join them on some important visits, but I was too busy doing other things. More focus by me on the teams outside would have helped them for sure. My sales manager reacted by stating that he should have spent more time on aligning with our marketing department around one of the new products we had launched. We had a good discussion, we both learned and we both improved. I focused on what I could do to improve, and my sales manager focussed on his own potential to improve.

▶

It takes a while before people understand my system, whereby I focus on my own improvement. In many cases, they are not used to a boss who constantly brings up his own mistakes. In the beginning, I got many reactions like: "Yeah, you're right, you made a mistake". However, after a while, people will start to copy your behaviour and focus on their own improvement.

Introducing this kind of vulnerability in a company that isn't used to it is not easy. You have to fight through the first phase. However, in the end, people have always followed me, by starting to change themselves, to focus on personal improvements instead of trying to change others.

You are the leader, you set the tone of voice. If you are able to show your vulnerability, to focus on the things that might improve you, your people will show themselves vulnerable as well. Vulnerability increases the speed of improvement in a company.

Q: How do you strike the balance between being tough and being vulnerable?

"Looking for the problem behind the problem reduces the need to compromise"

44. Cut down on compromises

I doubt whether compromises are useful. Personally, I try not to compromise. On the few occasions in the past when I have compromised, the agreement we made did not turn out to be successful. When two parties who are trying to make a deal agree to be open about why they do or do not agree with the reasoning of the other party, it is rarely necessary to compromise.

During my time working on mergers and acquisitions, I negotiated a lot, each time with different parties. Drafting a contract to buy a company is a very complex thing. There is mostly big money at stake and the parties involved often do not know each other very well. In these deals, there are many items (risks) that each party would like to have covered. Due to the fact the dealing parties are often dealing with each other for the first time, the reasoning behind specific issues is often unknown.

It helps a lot if you agree from the start to look for the problem behind the problem in case any issues arise (and you can be sure they will). The idea behind this is that by knowing the problem behind the problem, the number of possible solutions will multiply.

▶

There is this famous old example of two people fighting for one egg. They fight over it until they realise that one of them is only interested in the yoke, while the other only wants the white of the egg. Once both parties know why the other party wants the egg, the argument is resolved.

Once my company was buying a heating service company. The selling party wanted us to take over all the risks involved, including those related to issues that were not known by us at the time of the deal. We did not want that. We agreed to be open. We explained that we felt we could not handle the risks around old oil tanks standing on the company's premises as we had no experience with oil. They told us they were worried about possible legal implications with one of the company's customers. We had handled such legal situations before and felt comfortable taking over that particular risk. They felt comfortable taking over the risk of removing the oil tanks (there was a risk of polluting the premises, which would be costly to clean up).

By being open and transparent we came to an agreement without compromising. The same goes for many other situations where people get into trouble: a willingness to look for the problem behind the problem helps people to find solutions. The downside of compromising is that it shakes the foundations on which the relationship is built. People will not forget when they have compromised - especially since they often feel that they were the only one compromising. You will get into situations like: "Hey, last time I compromised, now it's your turn to compromise"...

I believe looking for the problem behind the problem reduces the need to compromise. Maximise interest-sharing by minimising position-based negotiation.

Q: Do you remember your last compromise? Still doesn't feel good, does it?

"Break-out meetings help new teams to align"

45. Your first break-out meeting with your new team

When a new leader wants to change the direction of a company, he/she needs to do so within the first one hundred days of taking the new position. Break-out meetings help new teams to align. I like to have a break out meeting with the team in the third month of a new job. We use the day to get to know each other better, to share the views on mission, vision, strategy, and our personal ambitions. We determine the agenda of the company and focus on team-building. Preferably, I ask a third party to act as a facilitator - someone who has lots of team-building experience. Last time we had such a break-out meeting, we used the following format:

Two weeks before the actual session, the facilitator presented an internet-driven tool called 'Management Drives'. Based on a short set of questions, this tool tries to predict what kind of person you are. There are many other tools that do it as well, and they all serve the purpose of facilitating a first-get together with a new team. One week before the session (after we had all filled out the test), our facilitator led us through the results of the test. During that meeting, we also discussed and finalised the agenda for the break-out meeting.

The break-out meeting started in the evening with cooking in a fish shop, where we had a quite a few drinks and laughs. The next morning we started by presenting ourselves to the group. We took thirty minutes each, in free format, except for the fact that talking about work was not allowed.

After that, we did a round of tips and compliments. Be careful, as a leader, you determine the tone of voice for the day, and if you do not start by presenting yourself in the morning in a very open, honest and vulnerable way, a round of tips and compliments might be premature.

After lunch, each individual presented his or her view on the vision, mission and strategy for our company. In the morning, I started presenting, in the afternoon I was the last to present. After the meeting, we had some internal meetings for fine-tuning what we presented, and one month later, we had a shared view on mission, vision, strategy. We were a team, all focused on continuous improvement, open to receive – and willing to give - constructive feedback. It is not always that easy, we were just lucky to have great people in the team.

Q: What is the name of the partner of each of your team members?

46

"I try to focus on a maximum of five key value drivers"

46. Focus

Focus on things that really add value. Being a manager, you can push many buttons, but take the time to think about which buttons you really want or need to push. Only a few things will really add value to your company, so focus on these things.

Within our company, every manager identifies his or her main key performance indicators (KPI) or value drivers. The KPI's are measured at least monthly. The many KPI's are collated in a scorecard with approximately fifteen KPI's for the whole company (see graph).

As a managing director, I also try to focus on a maximum of five value drivers. These value drivers differ for each company and might change within a company from time to time. I am currently focusing on debt collection, customer retention, new business, customer satisfaction and employee satisfaction.

Example of balanced scorecard items (energy company)	
Financial (25%)	**Customers (25%)**
• EBIT	• Satisfaction - B2C
• Gross margin – Power	• Satisfaction - B2B
• Gross margin – Gas	• Retention
• Contracted margin next year	
• Maintenance cost of power plants	
Internal (25%)	**Employees (25%)**
• Availability of production park	• Dart rate (security)
• Maintenance hours	• Illness rate
• Number of successful innovations	• Satisfaction rate

Q: Which three value drivers are you focusing on at the moment?

"We have a hard time letting go of things that mean

a lot to us"

47. The next manager

When you become a manager, don't worry about the fact that your predecessor might not be too friendly towards you. Someone once told me that in business life you always have at least two enemies - the one who did the job before you and the one who will do the job after you. The person who did the job before you might not like the fact that you'll have different ideas about 'his' business. In the same way, you might not like the fact that the person after you will have different ideas about 'your' business. It is very hard not to feel offended by someone who has taken over your job.

In most cases it's totally unnecessary to feel bad about it, but it is a bit like someone is taking over your partner, and when you see them together, you'll have the feeling that they're having much more fun together than he/she and you had. What you don't see, or don't want to see, is that they will have issues as well, just like everybody else in the world. It is a strange thing in life that we have a hard time letting go of things that mean a lot to us.

It helps a lot to prepare the team and yourself for the next manager from the start, by sharing dreams and ambitions. Setting the agenda and being open about your ambition to take a next step, after you have completed your mission, helps your team and yourself prepare for the break-up. A good handover and a sort of ritual to close down on an important era in your life are helpful as well. Sometimes I haven't felt like having a farewell party, but I still feel bad about the times I moved on to a new job without having a small party.

Q: Do you remember the last time you stepped down without a farewell? How did it feel?

"You have more time than you think to prove yourself... take time to meet as many people as possible"

48. Your first weeks in a new company

The first weeks in your new role are extremely important. The employees will watch you very carefully. It is very tempting to make promises, but be careful with them – they are not always necessary. You have more time than you think to prove to people that you can add value. It is tempting to start giving an opinion on things, but again, be careful about doing so, you have more time than you think. It is tempting to start changing some things in the beginning.

There are many checklists for the first one hundred days. However, the most important thing in the first weeks is to meet as many people as possible. It is just like with moving to a new house: if you don't introduce yourself during the first weeks, you will be unlikely to have a relationship with the neighbours. When you do ring some bells, introducing yourself, people will always give you a warm welcome. The same goes for the people working in the local shops, and for the people within the company you have just started working for. Take time to meet as many people as possible, show your face and be as visible as possible. I try not to give an opinion on how things should be. There might be a good reason why things differ from one's last job. However, be curious.

▶

The tone of voice between you and your people is set during the first weeks. Be very aware of that before you go in. Make sure you have thought about what you want to share, and that you know what you want to learn, without getting less spontaneous. You might think about making a statement at the very start. I once started as a director in a company where I got the biggest room. Next to my office, eight people were packed into a similar-sized room. Together with the team manager in the other room, we decided to break down the wall, so they doubled their space and I went to another (much smaller) room. The impact of such a statement is the greatest when you make it at the start.

In addition to getting acquainted and connecting with people, I like to ask questions such as:

- "How can I help you to perform best?"
- "How do you think people perform best?"
- "Who are our five most important customers?"
- "How do we know whether our customers and our employees are happy?"
- "Which three things would you do if this were your company?"
- "Are you proud of your company?"
- "What would make you even prouder?" etcetera.

Your chances of creating the atmosphere necessary for continuous improvement are set in the first weeks. At the end of this book, there is a summary of all the questions of this book. They might help you to make a selection of the things you would like to ask people when you start a new job.

Q: What are the questions you would like to have

answered when starting a new job?

"You can only change yourself"

49. Change management

I see myself as a change manager since, amongst other things I am able to change myself. When people see that you are prepared to change yourself, when they see you're open to their thoughts, and when you really have the courage to take a vulnerable position, then people will start to change with you, and the company will change as a whole.

I have often heard managers standing before the troops saying: "we need to change". When they say "we", they really mean "you are all going to change". That approach has little chance of success in the current, complex western business world.

Despite seeing myself as a change manager, I do not like to talk about change. I prefer to talk about continuous improvement. When the competition is able to squeeze more margin out of their assets (assets being total resources, including the most important resource - the people), they are able to attract more funding or put lower prices out in the market. This worsens the position, the freedom and the fun of our company and the people in our company. Therefore, we try to improve continuously. We try to create a culture in which people start enjoying benchmarking their own performance against others, in- and outside of the company. They do this because they are convinced it leads to control over their own fate.

You can only improve continuously as a company when you, as a leader, are prepared to do likewise. You need to be very open to other people's vision. Make sure that the employees see your own change. Showing that you are learning is showing you are not perfect; admitting you were wrong. Why would your people admit they were wrong if you never do? They will only be willing to learn (change), if you are.

Last month, I got a big compliment from an ex-team member. He said that in his new job, he worked less hard than in our team, but that it took much more out of him. The reason for that was the lack of freedom and trust in his new team. The manager of the team was a very bossy person. For me, this compliment proves the philosophy is right. In a dream team, the coach is not the star player; he is just the one facilitating the team and making sure that they can be the stars.

Q: Are you trying to change others, or are you changing yourself?

"I doubt whether bonuses have a better effect on motivation than small pieces of in-kind recognition"

50. Employee of the month

In Europe, most people still see the American concept of giving an 'employee of the month' award as being a bit over the top. However, in my company, we decided a while ago to pay more attention to exceptional effort. We copied the American concept and poured a European sauce over it. We introduced the 'most customer-orientated employee' award. The award is not linked to a specific period, which gives some extra flexibility for the management, plus it doesn't feel over the top for the (European) employees.

When I started working with my current team as Managing Director, I had a private parking place. It was not as easy to reach as the parking places of our customers, but it still was the best parking place for an employee. We changed the licence plate marker for the MD on the sideboard into a marker saying 'most customer-orientated employee'.

Not long ago we nominated Gaby, an employee who had received a letter from one of our customers stating how happy she was with the service of our company, and with the help of Gaby in particular. Gaby always comes to the office by bicycle, so we installed a temporary bicycle rack for her on my old parking lot. I don't think I need to say how fast the story of the bike rack went through our office building. I doubt whether bonuses have a better effect on motivation than small pieces of in-kind recognition like this. It doesn't mean you shouldn't pay out bonuses, it just means there are more – and often more effective - ways to motivate your crew.

Q: What is your way to support extraordinary efforts by your employees?

"Make sure you know your weak spots, and gather people around you that fill in the competences you are missing"

51. Weak spots

Everybody has some weaker spots, even the most successful people. Make sure you know your weak spots, and gather people around you that fill in the competences you are missing. It can be very easy to find out what your weak spots are. You just have to make sure that you create an environment in which people are open to each other, and then ask your team members. They know best where your weak or blind spots are. But remember, knowing your weak spots is nothing more than knowing your weak spots in the situations you have coped with so far. New situations might mean discovering new weak spots, so make sure you keep asking for feedback. We are never too old to learn.

Strong negative feedback is not always nice. As a leader, if you have created an open environment, you can be sure that you will get some strong feedback. Unfortunately, not every person can give 'advices' in a motivating and inspiring way, so it can be tough to hear. Nevertheless, it is important to ask lots of people how they think you could improve. I do not always feel comfortable asking for feedback. It's quite normal to be better at handling such 'advice' when you feel strong. However, at least during evaluation rounds, I strongly believe you have to ask for tips to improve yourself.

When things are not going smoothly in your team, at least two people have something to improve: you and one of your direct reports. To the outside world, you take the blame for failures and the team gets all the credits. Therefore, you get the highest salary. By doing so, you win the right to be critical towards your team members internally. As the leader, you have to earn the right to be critical towards your team.

When I'm talking to someone in my team about something that has gone wrong, I always start by saying what I could have done better myself. This is an invitation for my counterpart to tell what he or she might have done better. It does not matter who made the bigger mistake, it's about the willingness of each person to improve on a continuous basis.

▶

One of my main weak spots (and I know it is a familiar weak spot for managers), is that I tend to hire people like me (enthusiastic, open, honest, like to have some laughs, general management type). However, this means, I tend to forget that a company also needs people who understand the detailed specifics of business we're in :-) I once discussed this very openly with the team, and we decided to form a team around me to test new job-candidates on their in-depth knowledge of the field we work in.

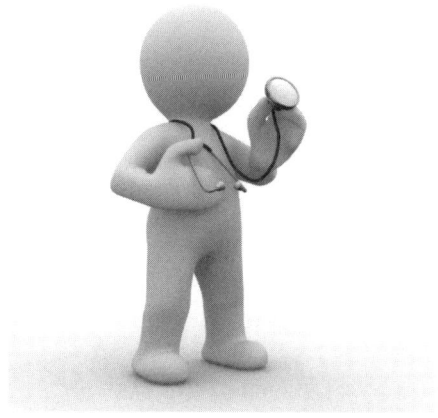

Q: Who complements your weak spot(s)?

52

"Quick reactions are at least as important outside as inside a company"

52. Complaint handling

Quick reactions are at least as important outside as inside a company. Take complaint handling, for example, which for many different reasons takes too much time in many different companies. In my company, in the old days when a complaint came in, we used to send a letter to the customer, stating we had received the complaint. In the letter, we promised to take 10 days for follow up. This letter was sometimes followed by a second letter, stating that, unfortunately, it would take another 10 days to resolve the complaint.

This was a long process and our complainants were not happy with it, so we decided to change our approach. Now, we give the customer a simple call on the day the complaint comes in, just to confirm that we have received the complaint and to check if we have understood the issue correctly. In this initial phone call, the customer gets a personal apology for the fact that things went wrong. It doesn't matter if the employee making the call was involved in the mistake, or whether it was only our fault. This phone call is followed by a 'thank you' for the fact that the customer took the effort to write a note instead of leaving us for the competition. In many cases, we solve the issue in the first call. We now understand our customers better and customer satisfaction has improved.

Q: How does your complaint process work?

53

53. Take a break once in a while

Over the years, many people have told me that my way of working with groups is unusual. This year a colleague told me that I should try to put my way of working onto paper. I liked the idea from the beginning, and I am happy that my employer (Essent / RWE) has allowed me to spend time doing so. I always wanted to write and produce something permanent. However, although writing is a marvellous way to structure my thoughts, it's hard for me to do something on my own. Through writing, I have learnt that I'm a real team player, I don't like to be on my own, and I need the team.

Before I started this book, I set myself a target of 53 columns. Most management books I read so far, I have just scanned through, between meetings or on a plane. I mostly only remember one or two things from these books, probably just because I read too fast. I wanted to write a book which invites the reader to read slowly. I chose the 53 columns concept, so one can read a column per week and discuss with friends, peers or the team. I hope some or all of the columns will have inspired you to try something new, and will help you, your people and your company on the way to a self-steering, continuously-improving, a high performance organisation.

To write these columns, I had a room with a view, looking out on the north face of the Matterhorn in Switzerland. I wrote this book in a chalet called La Pente, in a village called Les Collons (at an altitude of 1800m). It's a fantastic place to take a break, to calm down from working, to go for a walk or go skiing, to drink wine in front of a beautiful fireplace, or have a Swiss cheese fondue high up in the mountains. For me this was a fantastic place to structure my thoughts. Sharing the insights that I have gathered over the last twelve years, gives a lot of positive energy.

Composing these columns has enabled me to free up my mind and to recharge my batteries. I now feel ready for new adventures, for meeting new teams, and for finding new improvements to myself and the world around me.

Q: When was the last time you took a break to recharge and structure your thoughts?

Some questions to ask

1: Who would you go to to share your insights?

2: How do you show your direct reports that you trust them?

3: Where does each of your team members want to be in three years' time?

4: How do you motivate people to get from A to B?

5: Would you determine the percentage of strongest and weakest players in your team?

6: Does your boss know your career aspirations?

7: How do you ensure you are visible enough?

8: How would you involve your key stakeholders when solving a crisis?

9: Who are the over- and under-performers in your company/team?

10: How would you set up an all hands meeting?

11: What percentage of your customers contributes 80% to your profitability?

12: How do you enable your people to improve themselves continuously?

13: How are you currently working on the least profitable part of your business?

14: Which customer would you invite to join one of your meetings?

15: What would be the top five questions you would ask your customer?

16: Do you spend your time on the things you really need to?

17: Would your employees say you never forget a thing?

18: How often do you use three arguments to stress your opinion?

19: Do you act the part of a leader or a manager?

20: Do you feel resistance to bringing stakeholders together in person? If so, why?

21: To which person would you present your idea as someone else's?

22: Who would you ask to help you fire up your team?

23: What would you change if the company you work for were yours?

24: Does your ranking process improve the performance of your company?

25: How many emails lie in your inbox unanswered for more than 24 hours?

26: What was the difference in your reaction between your latest drawback and your first?

27: When was the last time you did not listen to your intuition? Do you still regret it?

28: How long do you think it should take before new employee feels at home?

29: Did you ever need a coach in teams where there was already a high level of trust?

30: Who would you ask to come up with a plan to spice up the office interior?

31: How do you prepare for evaluations of your staff?

32: Are you sure all your activities are adding value to your bottom line?

33: What would you do if a team did not accept its leader?

34: How much knowledge do you externalise by hiring consultants?

35 Do you think business relationships differ strongly from private relationships?

36: What was your dream back at school?

37: What is your company's reason for being (one sentence)?

38: What would be your ctrl-alt-delete sport?

39: Do you have an example of a successful relationship where there was no trust?

40: Do you know the dreams of your team?

41: What is your team's interpretation of the company's corporate values?

42: How do you stimulate smooth co-operation after a takeover?

43: How do you strike the balance between being tough and being vulnerable?

44: Do you remember your last compromise? Still doesn't feel good, does it?

45: What is the name of the partner of each of your team members?

46: Which three value drivers are you focusing on at the moment?

47 Do you remember the last time you stepped down without a farewell?
How did it feel?

48: What are the questions you would like to have answered when starting
a new job?

49: Are you trying to change others, or are you changing yourself?

50: What is your way to support extraordinary efforts by your employees?

51: Who complements your weak spot(s)?

52: How does your complaint process work?

53: When was the last time you took a break to recharge and structure
your thoughts?

Some special thank you's

Thank you so very much for reading this book. Please see this book as an invitation to share your experiences as well. Sharing forms the basis for growth.

Writing this book has been one of the greatest adventures in my life. It is impossible to thank all people that have contributed to this book.

However, I'd like to thank some people in particular. First, I'd like to thank my parents for teaching me the basic values in life, and my beloved wife Nina for the support she has given me during the process.

I want to thank my friend Sjaak for his idea to write this book and Alexis, who had great influence on the format. A special thanks to my friend Andreas for the cover and my friend Victoria for editing. Next to that, I'd like to thank all employees of Essent / RWE, and especially Erwin, for giving me the space to write this book.

Without my fantastic co-readers, this book would not been published at all. Thank you Nina, Rony, Henk, Friso, Klaus, Sergio, Klaas, Laurens, Niels, Bas, Jaap, Feike, Vincent, Nico, Jacqueline, Loek, Frans, Monica, Nico, Arjan, Charlotte, Lambert and Charlie.

In their own special way the following people also helped me: Janneke, Rob, Peter, Marcel, Jacob, Marc, Toon, Robert, Teun, Kees, Tonio, Jan, Friso, Ilse, Christ, Hans, Max, Rinse, Berend, Anouk, Olivier, Claus, Pauline, Merijn, Auke, Hans, René, Richard, Ben, Anita and Kim.

A very warm thank you to all the people I have had the chance to work with so far. Thanks for teaching me so much, and for making me the person that I am today.

MANAGING CAN BE SO EASY